Now I Know

What is a Fish

Written by David Eastman

Illustrated by Lynn Sweat

Troll Associates

Library of Congress Cataloging in Publication Data

Eastman, David.
    What is a fish.

    (Now I know)
    Summary: Describes different kinds of fish and where
and how they live.
      1. Fishes—Juvenile literature. [1. Fishes]
I. Sweat, Lynn, ill. II. Title.
QL617.2.E18   597   81-11373
ISBN 0-89375-660-1   AACR2
ISBN 0-89375-661-X (pbk.)

DOLPHIN

SHARK

10   9   8   7   6   5   4   3   2   1

What is a fish?

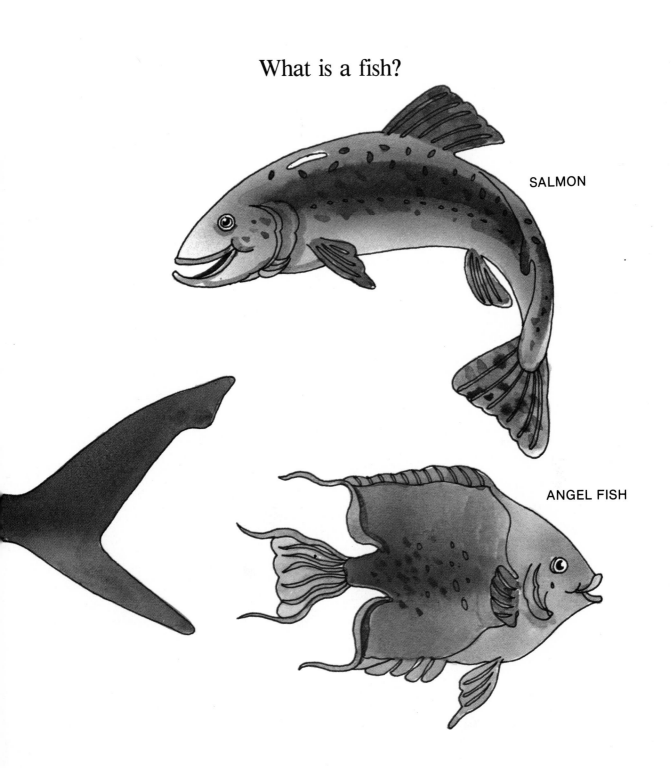

SALMON

ANGEL FISH

There are many kinds of fish.

There are sharks, catfish, and salmon . . . to name a few.

There are many sizes of fish.

A guppy and a goldfish are very small.

And a shark can be very big.

GILL

All fish have gills.

Gills help the fish breathe.

Most fish have fins to help them swim.

All fish live in water.

Most fish live in the ocean.
The ocean has salty water.

Other fish live in fresh water . . .
lakes, rivers, and streams.

PIKE

YELLOW PERCH

SUNFISH

CATFISH

There are many kinds of fish.

This is a swordfish. It can swim
very fast. It lives in the ocean.

A salmon can live in both salt and fresh water.

It is born in a stream, but usually spends most of its life in the ocean.

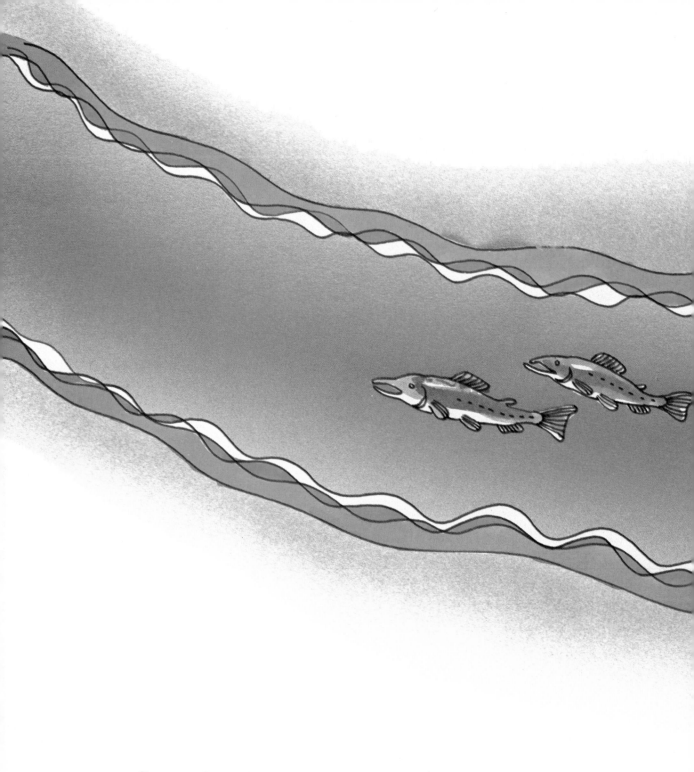

Later, it swims back to a stream to lay its eggs.

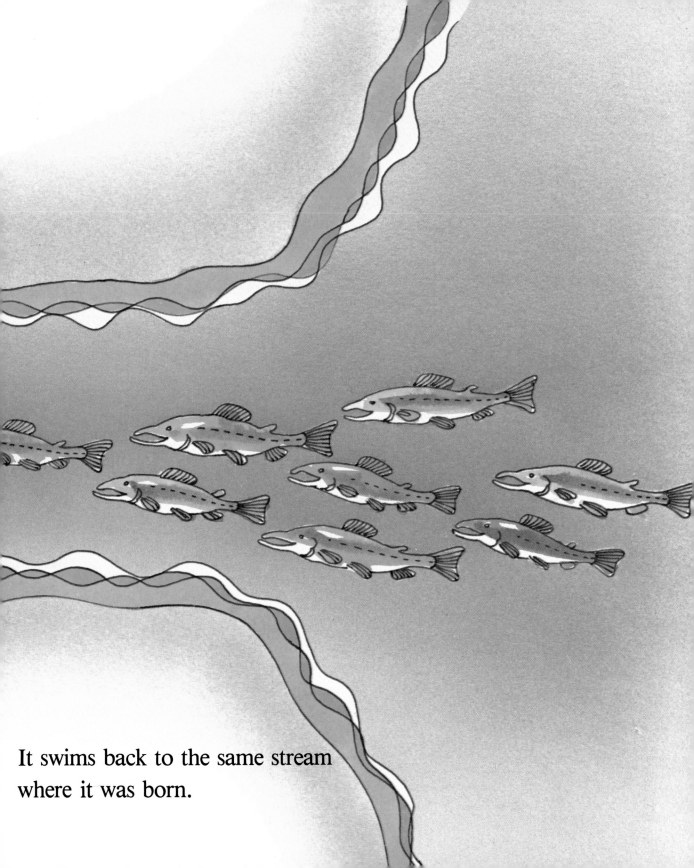

It swims back to the same stream
where it was born.

It is very hard for the salmon to swim up the stream.

Sometimes it will jump high over the water.

After the salmon lays its eggs,
it returns to the ocean.

Soon the baby salmon hatch. They,
too, will swim to the ocean to live.

TUNA

HALIBUT

Fish are in all the waters of the world.

MARLIN

JACK

GROUPER

They are in streams, lakes, and oceans . . .

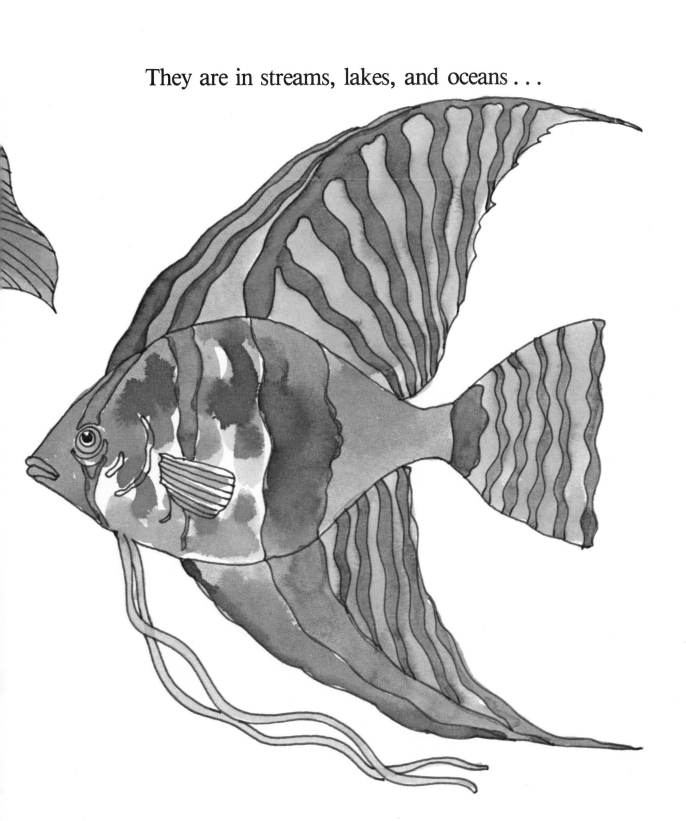

or even in your home!